1

Peas, Please!

Directions

1. Choose a word problem.
2. Place the peas on the plate to act out and solve the problem.

| There are 13 peas on the plate. You eat 5 peas. How many peas are left? | There are 15 peas on the plate. You eat 10 peas. Your mother puts 4 peas on the plate. How many peas do you have now? | There are 9 peas on the plate. Your mother puts 10 peas on the plate. You eat 12 peas. How many peas are left? | There are 7 peas on the plate. Your mother puts 8 peas on the plate. She adds 2 more peas. How many peas do you have now? | There are 18 peas on the plate. You eat 9 peas. You eat 3 more peas. How many peas are left? | There are 6 peas on the plate. Your father puts 8 peas on the plate. You eat 2 peas. How many peas are left? |

A Fine Line

You Will Need

• write-on/wipe-away marker

Directions

1. Place the problems facedown into three stacks by color.

2. Draw a problem from the first stack and place it on the mat. Make a number line on the wire to help you solve the problem.

3. Repeat with the next two stacks.

	15 + ☐ = 21	29 − ☐ = 18	☐ + 16 = 32	40 = ☐ + 10	25 = 32 − ☐
	There are 11 birds on the wire. Five birds join them. How many birds are there now?	There are 20 birds on the wire. Thirteen birds fly away. How many birds are left?	There are 9 birds on the wire. Six more birds join them. Two birds fly away. How many birds are left?	There are 33 birds on the wire. Eleven birds fly away. How many birds are left?	☐ − 9 = 8
	There are 10 birds on the wire. Twelve birds join them. How many birds are there now?	There are 46 birds on the wire. Eight birds fly away. Two birds come back. How many birds are there now?	Some birds are on the wire. 12 birds join them. Now, there are 19 birds. How many birds were on the wire?	Sixty birds are on the wire. Some more birds come. Now, there are 72 birds. How many birds came?	Some birds are on the wire. 18 birds fly away. Now, there are 34 birds. How many birds were on the wire?
			Forty birds are on the wire. Some more birds come. Now, there are 50 birds. How many birds came?	Some birds are on the wire. Two come. Eight come. Now, there are 53. How many birds were on the wire?	Eighty birds are on the wire. Some birds fly away. Now, there are 62 birds. How many birds flew away?

Kibble Count

Directions

1. Place a number on the large bowl. Place that number of dog food pieces in the bowl. Tell if the number is even or odd.

2. Divide the dog food pieces equally between Fido's bowl and Max's bowl. If there are no leftover pieces, the number is even. If there is one leftover piece, the number is odd.

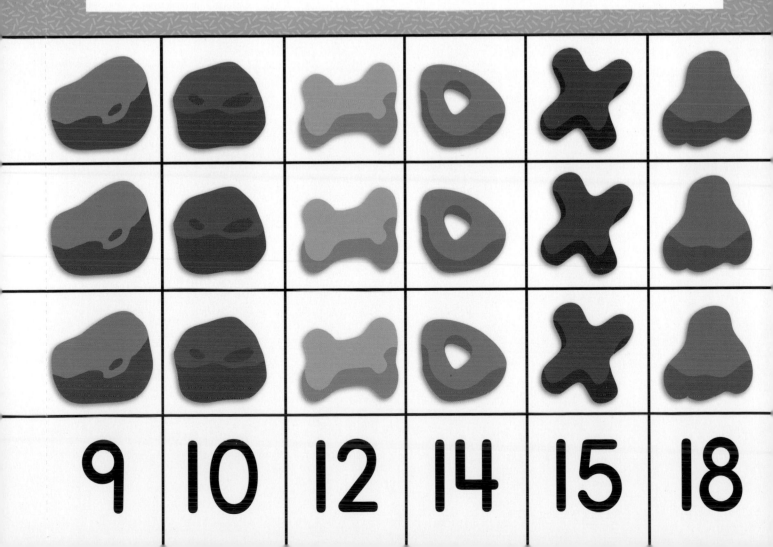

9 10 12 14 15 18

even

odd

even

odd

even

odd

even

odd

How Many Socks?

You Will Need

• write-on/wipe-away marker

Directions

1. Shuffle the cards and place them facedown in a stack.

2. The first player will choose a card and place it in the first row. The next player will choose a card and place it beside the first card. When a row is full, the next player up writes the number of socks and circles *odd* or *even*.

3. If only two players are playing, switch who goes first on the remaining rows.

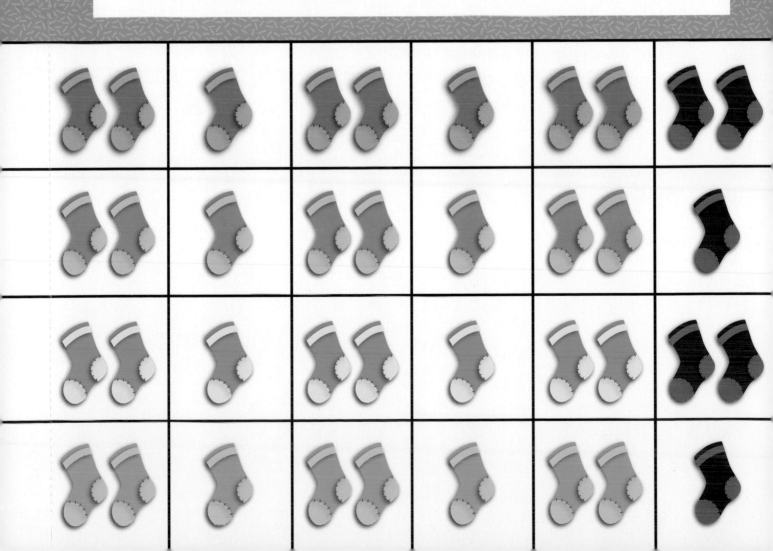

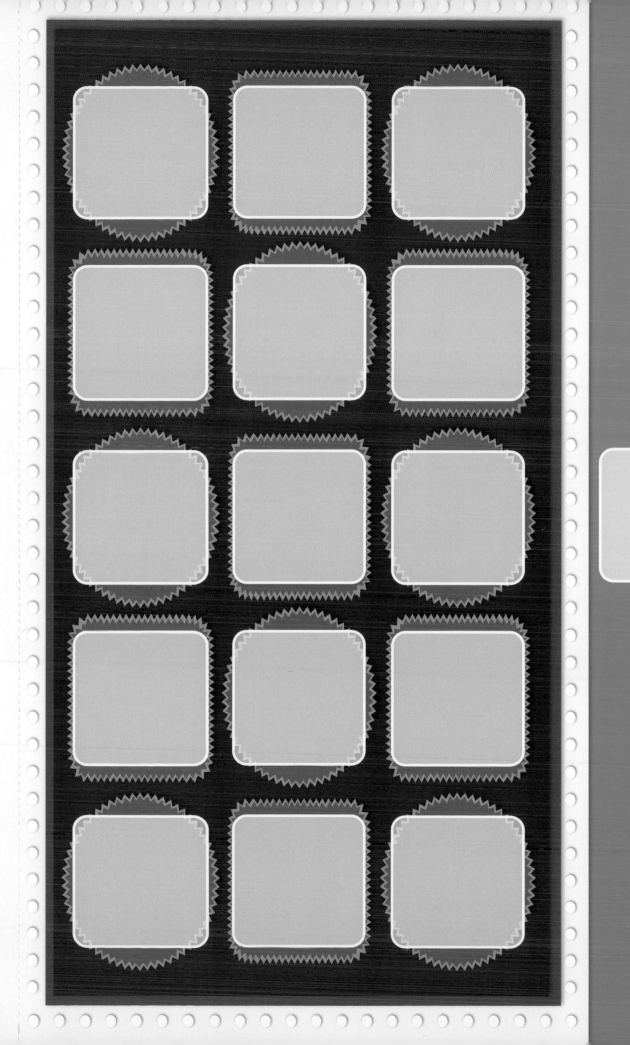

Sweet Arrays

Directions

1. Separate the chocolate cards from the equation cards and place them in two stacks.

2. Place an equation on the mat.

3. Use the chocolates to fill the box and create an array that matches the equation.

4. Tell the total number of chocolates.

| | | | 5 + 5 + 5 = ____ | 3 + 3 + 3 + 3 = ____ | 1 + 1 + 1 = ____ |
| 4 + 4 + 4 = ____ | 2 + 2 + 2 + 2 + 2 = ____ | 3 + 3 + 3 = ____ | 4 + 4 = ____ | 2 + 2 + 2 + 2 = ____ | 1 + 1 + 1 + 1 + 1 = ____ |

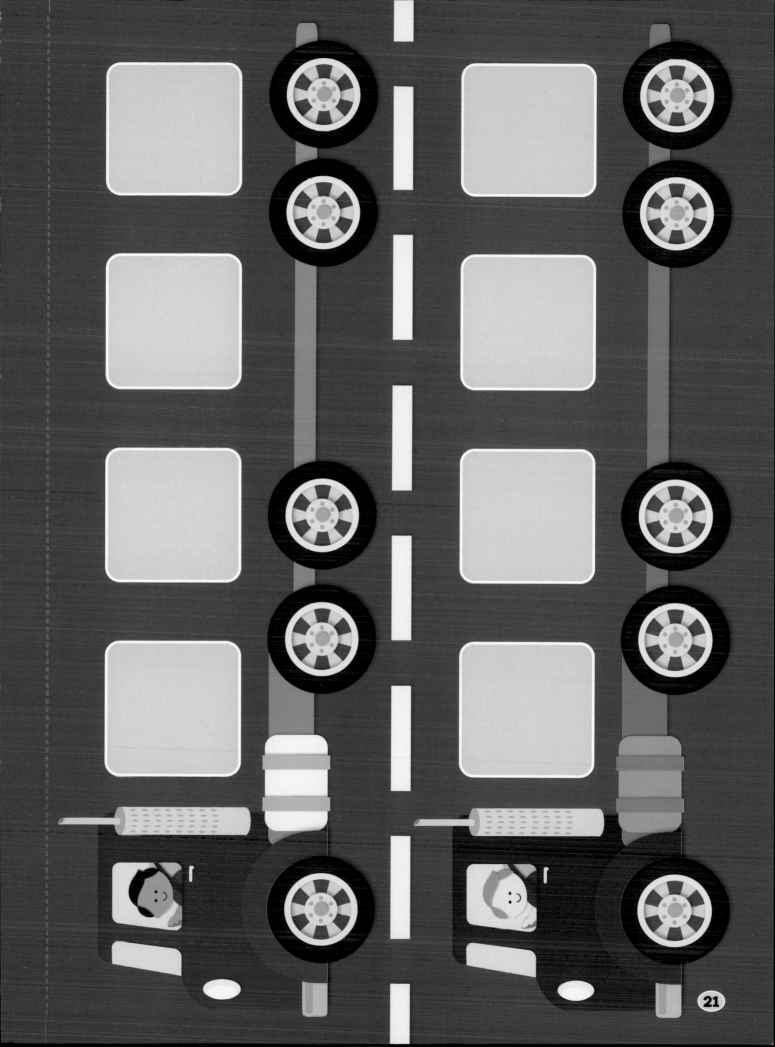

Number Haul

Directions

1. Place the numbers facedown in a stack.

2. Each player takes a turn drawing a number and placing it on his truck bed.

3. The winner is the player with the greatest number.

■ Variation: Players use the numbers to try to make the smallest number.

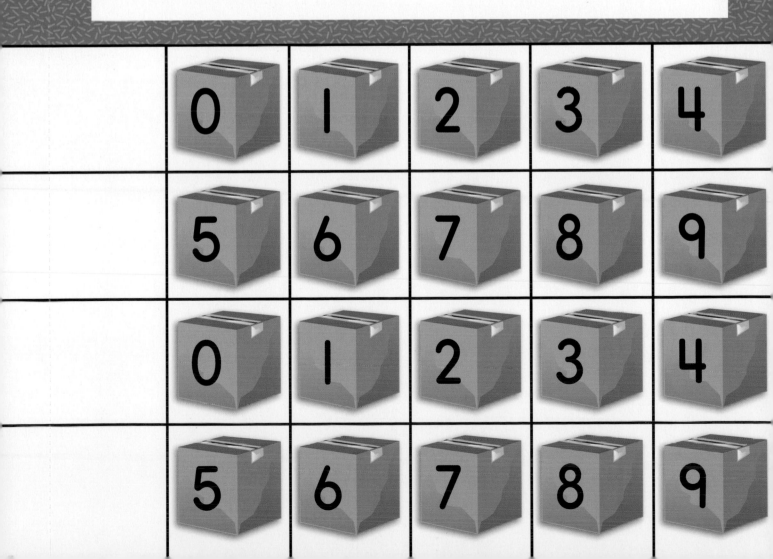

Thousand Chart

10	20	30	40	50	60	70	80	90	100
110	120	130	140	150	160	170	180	190	200
210	220	230	240	250	260	270	280	290	300
310	320	330	340	350	360	370	380	390	400
410	420	430	440	450	460	470	480	490	500
510	520	530	540	550	560	570	580	590	600
610	620	630	640	650	660	670	680	690	700
710	720	730	740	750	760	770	780	790	800
810	820	830	840	850	860	870	880	890	900
910	920	930	940	950	960	970	980	990	1000

Hundred Chart

1	2	3	4	5	6	7	8	9	10
11	12	13	14	15	16	17	18	19	20
21	22	23	24	25	26	27	28	29	30
31	32	33	34	35	36	37	38	39	40
41	42	43	44	45	46	47	48	49	50
51	52	53	54	55	56	57	58	59	60
61	62	63	64	65	66	67	68	69	70
71	72	73	74	75	76	77	78	79	80
81	82	83	84	85	86	87	88	89	90
91	92	93	94	95	96	97	98	99	100

Noteworthy Numbers

You Will Need

• write-on/wipe-away marker

Directions

1. Place the cards facedown in a stack.

2. Choose a card.

3. Use the correct chart to answer the question or color the pattern.

	Count by 5s, starting at 50.	Count by 10s, starting at 10.	Count back by 5s, starting at 50.	Count by 100s, starting at 100.	Count by 10s, starting at 500.
	Count back by 10s, starting at 500.	What are the next three numbers after 548?	What are the next three numbers after 621?	What are the next three numbers after 288?	What are the next three numbers after 89?
	What are the next three numbers after 104?	When you count back from 301, what three numbers do you say?	When you count back from 87, what three numbers do you say?	When you count back by 10s from 100, what three numbers do you say?	When you count back by 10s from 880, what three numbers do you say?
	When you count back by 5s from 55, what three numbers do you say?	When you count back by 100s from 900, what three numbers do you say?			

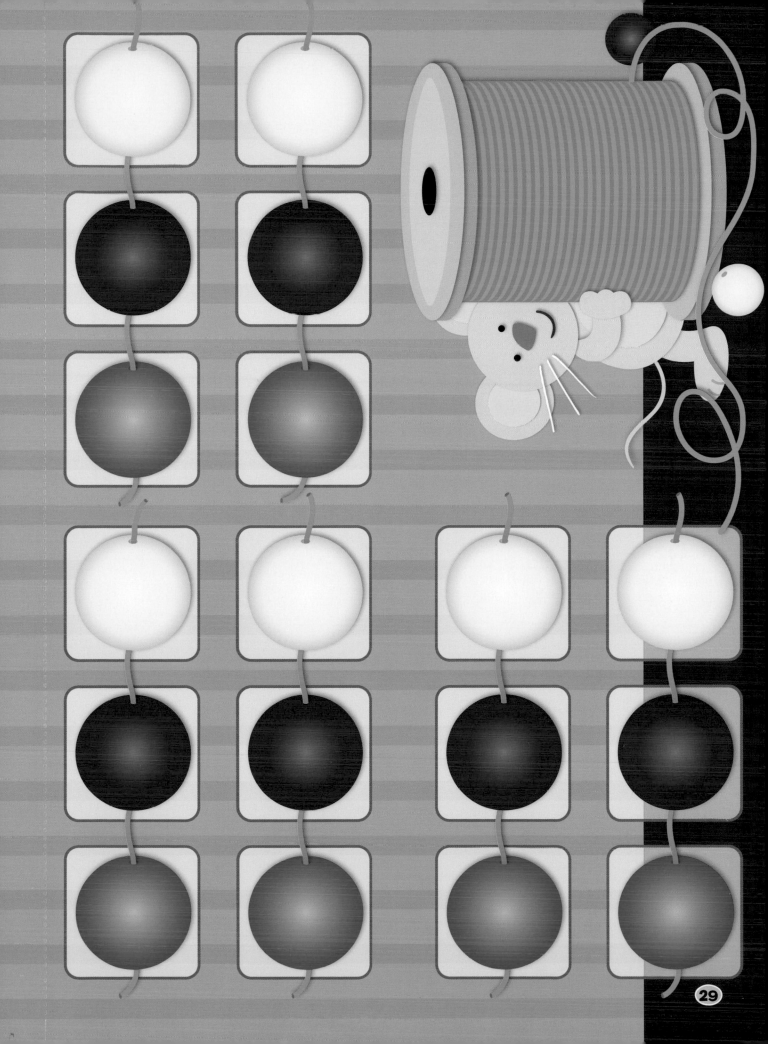

Expand-a-Strand

Directions

1. Place the cards facedown into three stacks by color.

2. Draw a card from each stack. Place each card in the matching spaces on the first string of beads. Repeat with the remaining strings of beads.

3. Flip over the cards to see their values. Tell the expanded form of each number made.

1	2	3	4	5	6
7	8	1	2	3	4
5	6	7	8	1	2
3	4	5	6	7	8

6 5 4 3 2 1

40 30 20 10 8 7

200 100 80 70 60 50

800 700 600 500 400 300

Number Know How

You Will Need

- write-on/wipe-away marker

Directions

1. Lay aside the 4 number cards. Shuffle the remaining cards and place them facedown in rows. Place one of the number cards in the yellow circle.

2. The first player will turn over a card. If it matches the number card, he places it in a circle and goes again. If not, the card is turned over and the other player takes a turn. The player to fill the final circle takes all the cards.

3. Play continues with each of the other numbers.

|||| |||| |||| |||| ||||	$\begin{array}{r} 10 \\ 10 \\ +\ 5 \\ \hline \end{array}$	25¢		**25**
|||| |||| |||| |||| |||| |||| |||| ||	$\begin{array}{r} 65 \\ -\ 23 \\ \hline \end{array}$	10¢ 10¢ 10¢ 10¢ 1¢ 1¢		**42**
|||| |||| |||| |||| |||| |||| |||| |||| |||| |||| |||| |||| |||| ||||		$\begin{array}{r} 35 \\ +41 \\ \hline \end{array}$	25¢ 25¢ 25¢ 1¢		**76**
|||| |||| |||| |||| |||| |||| |||| |||| |||| |||| |||| |||| |||| |||| |||| |||| |||| |||| |||| ||||	$\begin{array}{r} 63 \\ +37 \\ \hline \end{array}$	$1		**100**

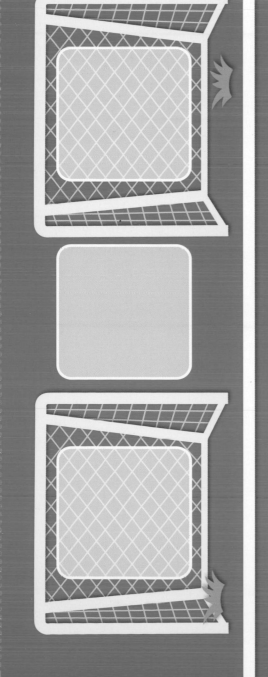

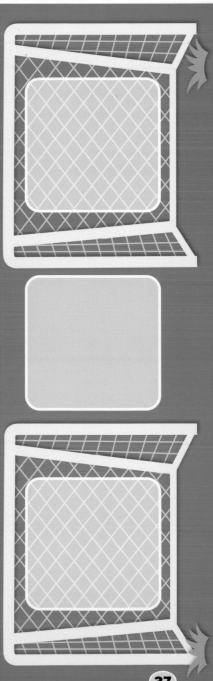

Greater Goals

You Will Need

• write-on/wipe-away marker

Directions

1. Choose two numbers and place them on the first set of goals. Use a symbol to compare the numbers.

2. Show how you know on the whiteboard. Repeat these steps for the next two sets of goals.

452	425	740	840	636	963
293	301	498	488	187	184
548	845	901	919	>	>
>	<	<	<	=	=

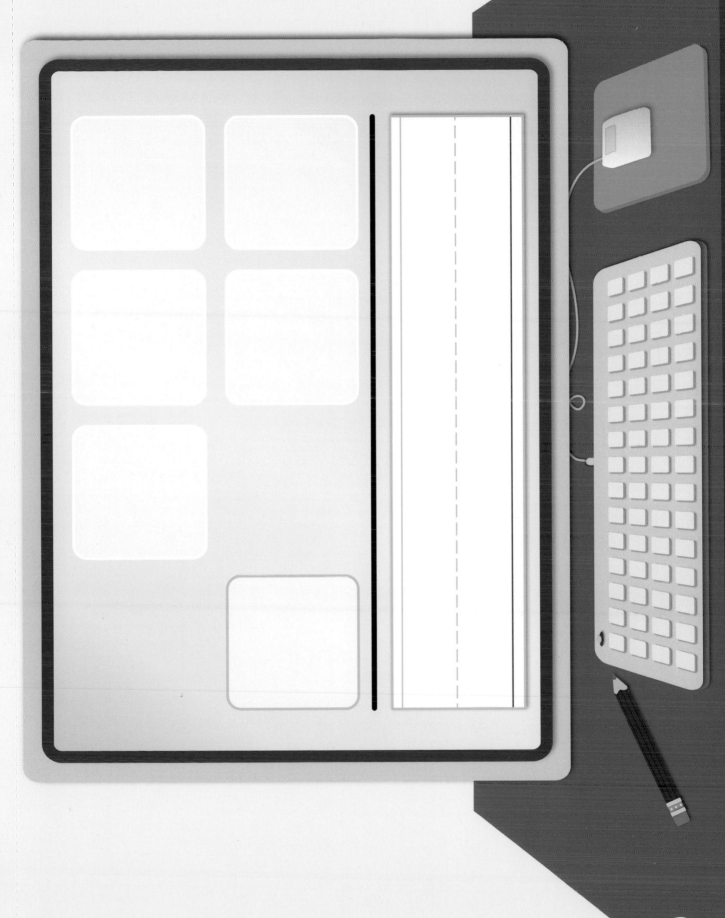

Programming Problems

You Will Need

• write-on/wipe-away marker

Directions

1. Place the numbers facedown in a stack.

2. Draw five numbers and place them in the spaces on the mat.

3. Place a plus sign or a minus sign in the blue-outlined space. Solve the problem. Write the answer.

0	1	2	3	4	5
6	7	8	9	0	1
2	3	4	5	6	7
8	9	+	−		

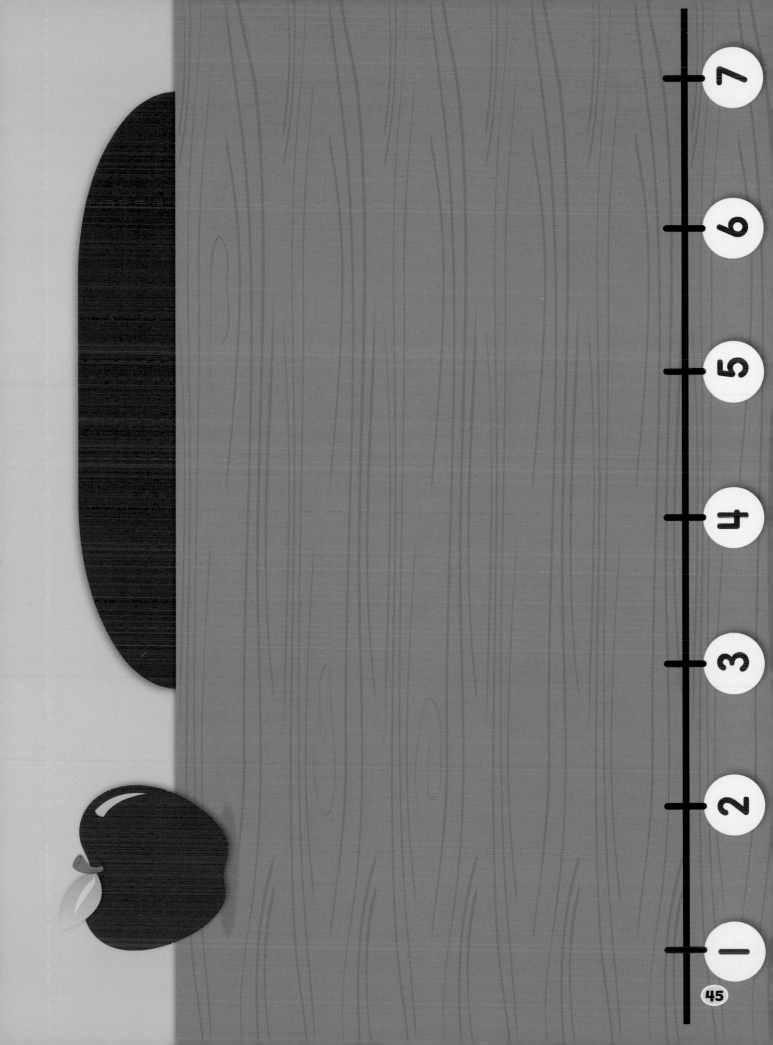

School Tools

Directions

1. Your teacher measured all of the items on her desk. The items are shown on the cards. Choose 10 items.

2. Plot each item on the line plot. Tell what you notice about the data.

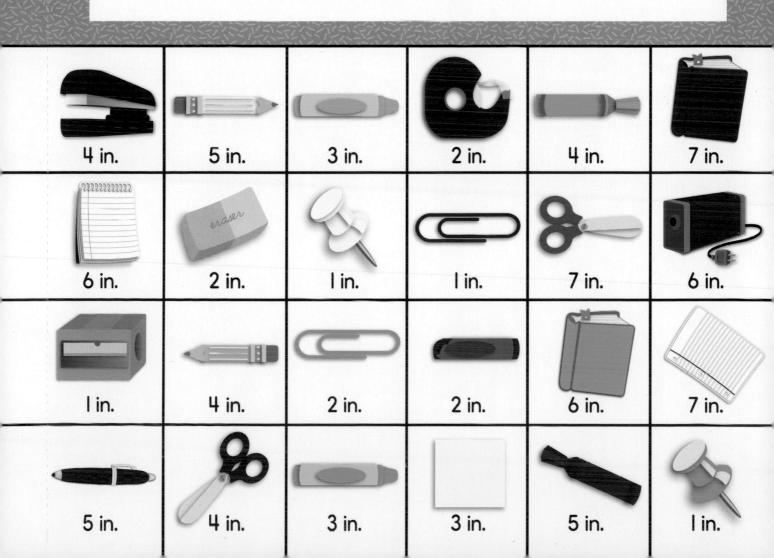

4 in.	5 in.	3 in.	2 in.	4 in.	7 in.
6 in.	2 in.	1 in.	1 in.	7 in.	6 in.
1 in.	4 in.	2 in.	2 in.	6 in.	7 in.
5 in.	4 in.	3 in.	3 in.	5 in.	1 in.

Team	Wins
Eagles	|||
Orioles	~~||||~~ ||
Cardinals	||||
Ravens	~~||||~~

Ravens

Cardinals

Orioles

Eagles

Game-Day Graphing

Directions

1. Read the data.

2. Create a picture graph with the baseballs.

3. Tell what you notice about the graph.

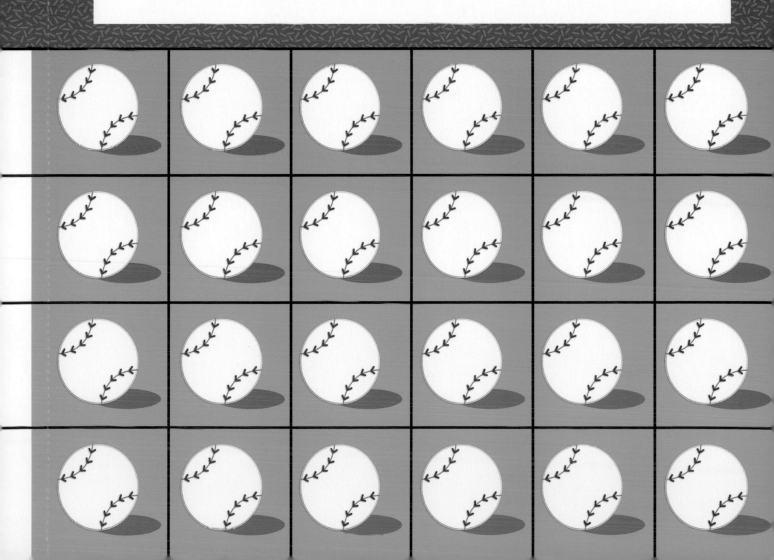

Tick-tock on the Clock

You Will Need

• write-on/wipe-away marker

Directions

1. Place the times facedown in a stack. Choose one time and draw the hands on the first clock to show the time.

2. Choose another time and draw the hands on the second clock to show the time.

■ Challenge: Tell how much time has passed between the first time and the second time.

4:15	5:35	7:10	8:40	11:50	1:05
3:20	6:30	1:45	2:15	6:20	7:55
5:55	4:25	8:10	9:05	9:30	10:50
10:20	12:40	1:45	2:35	12:10	2:40

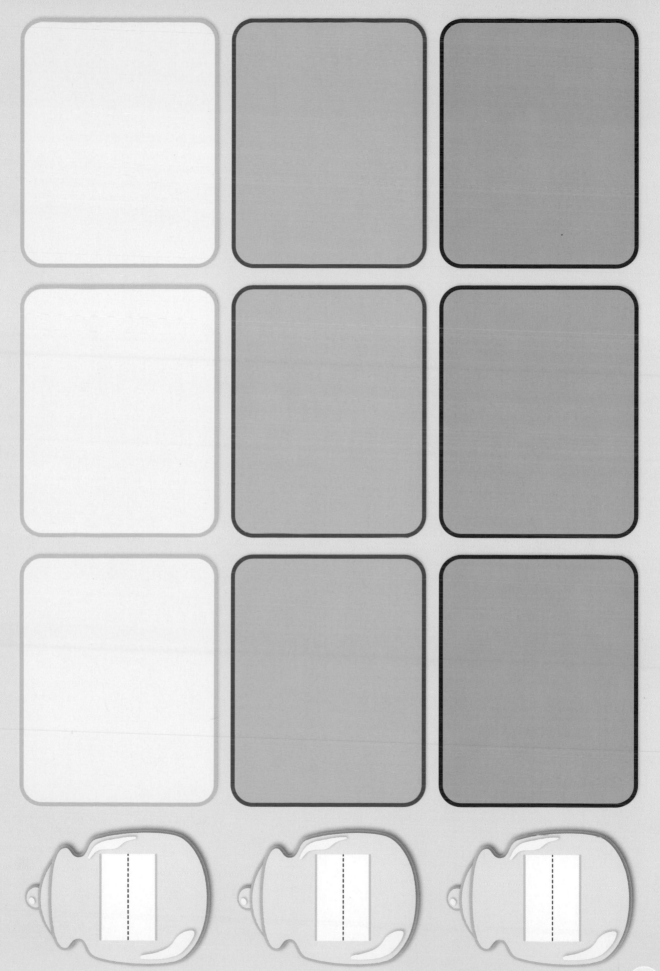

Money Jars

You Will Need

• write-on/wipe-away marker

Directions

1. Shuffle the money cards and place them facedown in a stack.

2. The first player will turn over a money card. As each player takes a turn, she will place the card in the consecutive square and count how much money it is.

3. When all three squares are filled, the next player will count all of the money and write the amount in the jar.

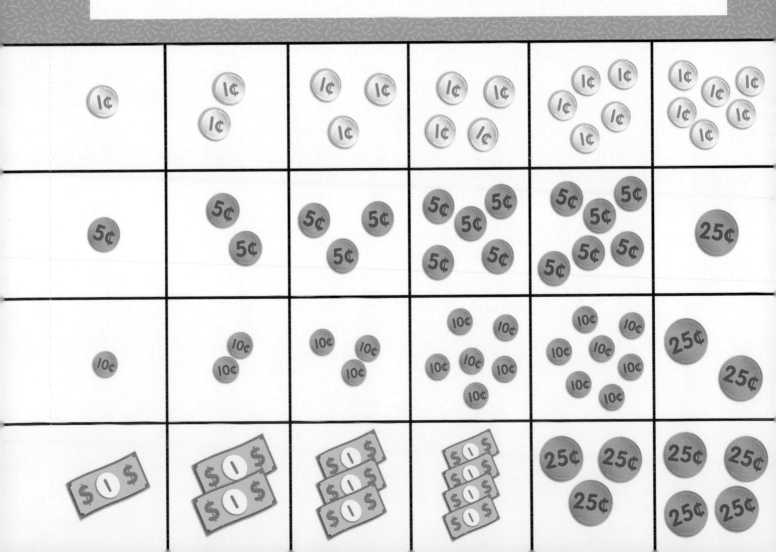

More Than $1.00

Less Than $1.00

Money Matters

Directions

1. Place the word problems in a stack. Spread out the money pictures.

2. Choose a word problem and estimate the answer. Place it on the correct coin purse.

3. Solve each problem. Match the money pictures to the correct problems.

Madison saved $5.00 to spend in the bookstore. She bought a book that cost $3.25. What was her change?	Perry had $2.00. He bought 3 packs of cards for $1.77. What was his change?	Kami bought a CD at the store for $6.88. She handed the cashier a ten-dollar bill. How much change did she receive?	Mark bought a video for $1.40. He paid with a five-dollar bill. How much change did he receive?	A baseball glove cost $3.98. Justin paid with a ten-dollar bill. How much change did he receive?	Mark sold his toy car to Leo. If Mark gave Leo $0.67 in change from a five-dollar bill, how much was Mark selling his toy cars for?
Whitney bought a vase. She handed the cashier a twenty-dollar bill. The vase was on sale for $9.98. What was her change?	Ben bought fruit for $5.25. He bought bananas for $2.02, apples for $2.51, and pears for some more. How much were the pears?	Zoe paid $1.25 for a pack of stickers. Her friend Chloe paid $1.69 for a pack of stickers. How much more did Chloe pay than Zoe?	Mr. Murphy sold a chair for $33.65. The customer paid with 2 twenty-dollar bills. How much change did Mr. Murphy give her?	Trey wants to buy a skateboard that costs $46.98. He has saved $50.00. How much money will he have left?	Mr. Novak gave the cashier a twenty-dollar bill for his groceries. His change was $12.38. How much did his groceries cost?

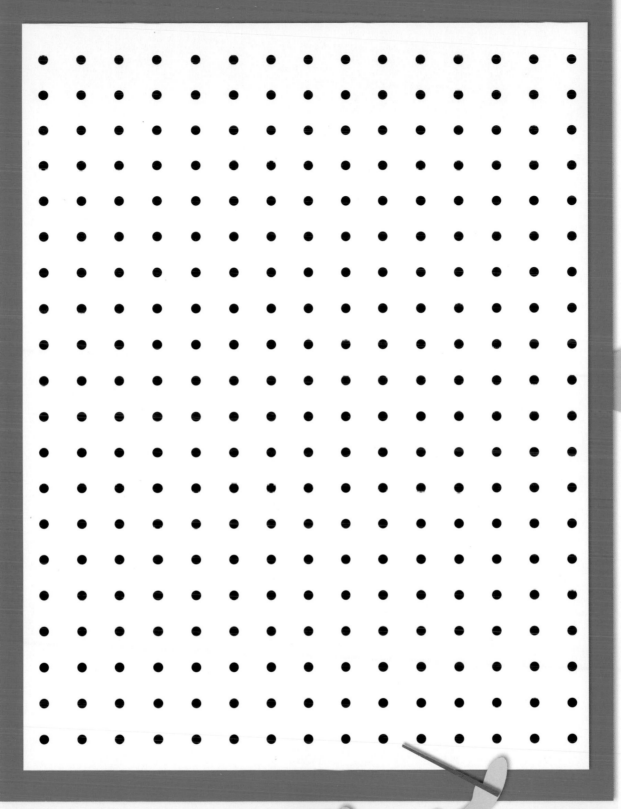

Square Off!

You Will Need

- write-on/wipe-away markers in two different colors

Directions

1. Place the cards facedown in a stack. Take turns choosing a card and drawing the rectangle.

2. Inside your rectangle, write how many square units make up the rectangle.

3. To win, create non-overlapping rectangles with the most square units.

1 row by 1 column	1 row by 2 columns	1 row by 3 columns	1 row by 4 columns	1 row by 5 columns	2 rows by 1 column
2 rows by 2 columns	2 rows by 3 columns	2 rows by 4 columns	2 rows by 5 columns	3 rows by 1 column	3 rows by 2 columns
3 rows by 3 columns	3 rows by 4 columns	3 rows by 5 columns	4 rows by 1 column	4 rows by 2 columns	4 rows by 3 columns
4 rows by 4 columns	4 rows by 5 columns	5 rows by 1 column	5 rows by 2 columns	5 rows by 3 columns	5 rows by 4 columns

six sides

two faces

no angles

six faces

three angles

Angles, Faces, and Sides

You Will Need

• write-on/wipe-away marker

Directions

1. Deal 5 cards facedown to each player. Make a discard pile with the remaining cards. Players can lay down any pairs they have on the row that fits the description.

2. The youngest player will start by asking the other player if she has a _____. If so, she must give it up. If the first player can make a pair, he will lay it on the correct row.

3. If the player does not have the requested card, the first player takes a card from the discard pile. The game continues, switching players, until one player is out of cards.

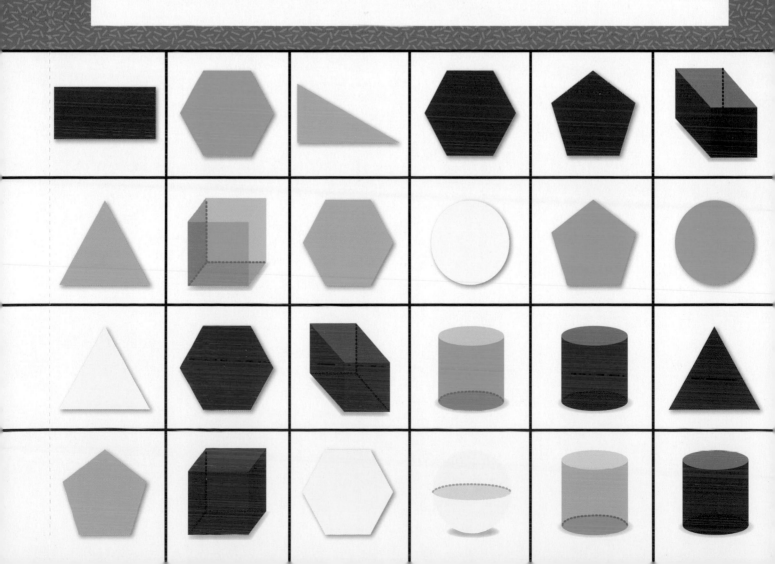

Piece of Cake

You Will Need

• write-on/wipe-away marker

Directions

1. Place the shape and fraction words into two stacks.

2. Draw one word at a time from each stack. Place them on the mat.

3. Find a cake in the bakery that matches the shape and divide it into the correct number of pieces with a write-on/wipe-away marker.

rectangle	rectangle	rectangle	rectangle	square	square
square	square	circle	circle	circle	circle
halves	halves	halves	halves	thirds	thirds
thirds	thirds	fourths	fourths	fourths	fourths

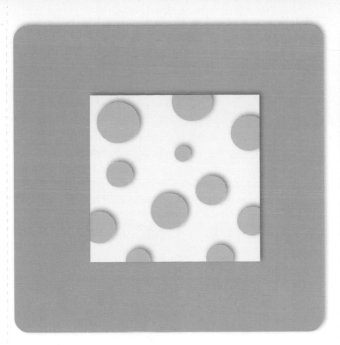

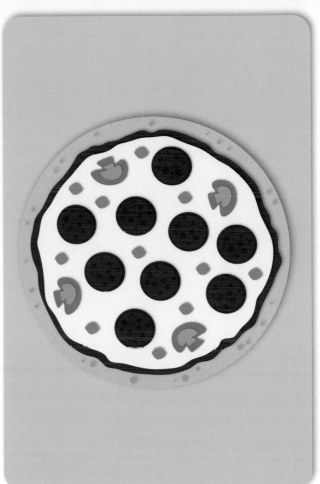

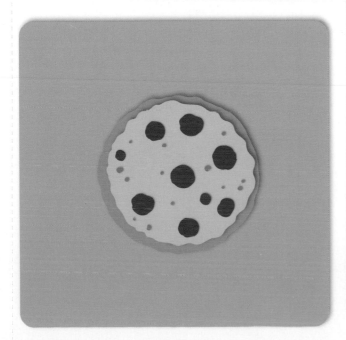

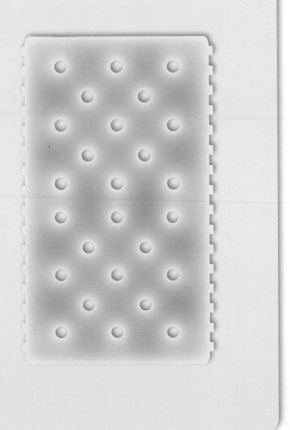

Fraction Snacks

You Will Need

• write-on/wipe-away marker

Directions

1. Shuffle the cards and divide them in half for each of two players. Roll a die to see which player goes first.

2. The first player uses a write-on/wipe-away marker to divide one item in half, thirds, or quarters. He may then place any cards that match that fraction on the snack tray.

3. The second player places any matching cards on the first player's snack tray. Then, she uses a write-on/wipe-away marker to divide another item in half, thirds, or quarters. She may then place any cards that match that fraction on the snack tray.

4. The game continues until one player is out of cards.

quarters	halves	thirds	a half of	a third of	a quarter of
$\dfrac{1}{2}$	quarters	halves	thirds	a half of	a third of
$\dfrac{1}{2}$	$\dfrac{1}{2}$	$\dfrac{1}{2}$	$\dfrac{1}{3}$	$\dfrac{1}{3}$	a quarter of
$\dfrac{1}{4}$	$\dfrac{1}{3}$	$\dfrac{1}{4}$	$\dfrac{1}{4}$	$\dfrac{1}{4}$	$\dfrac{1}{4}$